AF316950

Poetry and Thoughts

POETRY

and

THOUGHTS

Throughout My Years

Mildred Thayer Carneal

Copyright © 2023 by Mildred Thayer Carneal

All rights reserved. No part of this publication may be reproduced, distributed, or transmitted in any form or by any means, including photocopying, recording, or other electronic or mechanical methods, without the prior written permission of the copyright owner or the publisher, except in the case of brief quotations embodied in critical reviews and certain other noncommercial uses permitted by copyright law. For permission requests, write to the publisher, addressed "Attention: Permissions Coordinator," at the address below.

ARPress
45 Dan Road Suite 5
Canton MA 02021

Hotline: 1(888) 821-0229
Fax: 1(508) 545-7580

Ordering Information:
Quantity sales. Special discounts are available on quantity purchases by corporations, associations, and others. For details, contact the publisher at the address above.

Printed in the United States of America.

ISBN-13:   Softcover   979-8-89330-421-3
                eBook   979-8-89330-422-0

Library of Congress Control Number: 2024901011

TABLE OF CONTENTS

Preface

When I was a very young girl our mother would "tell" us the story of the ancient mariner ("The Rime of the Ancyent Marinere" by Samuel Taylor Coleridge, published in 1798 in *Lyrical Ballads*). As the youngest in our family, I could not help but wonder if the others understood any better than I did what the words meant that our mother was so dramatically relating to us. I caught some of it, enough to know it was about a sailor and what his travels had meant to him and that he was trying to tell his story to another, less interested person.

Time went on and I started school and learned about poetry: how to put it together, how to rhyme, and how to carry the meaning along. I thought back to the ancient mariner and wondered how any poet could carry the whole process for so long, with such big words, big thoughts, and complicated word illustrations.

I began writing poetry around the third grade. My decision on what type of poetry I would like to write was based on different things: the fact that I was eight or nine years old; that I had listened to my mom recite many, many long and difficult poems; that I had an inner desire to help others enjoy poetry; and that I had a God-given ability to take huge thoughts and transform them into simple-to-understand poems.

These are my poems and thoughts written over fifty-eight years, from 1954 to 2012. Even though they are easy to read they are sometimes laced with underlying messages relative to present life situations. I hope you enjoy and can relate to my poems and other short thoughts in a way that uplifts your spirits and gives you clearer meanings of joy, love, passion, simplicity, pain, life, and, most of all, God and His Bible.

Mildred Thayer Carneal

Dedication

To my mom and dad and entire family, those who are related and those adopted, those immediate and those who are distant, without whom I would never have had the life experiences that provided many of my opinions, thoughts, and expressions in this book.

Especially to my husband, Ed, and to my children, and my grandchildren, who have given me love, time, fun, courage, and laughter, things a writer cannot do without. My children and their families include Tara, Mason, Madison, and Gabriel; Shawn, Cody, Brady and Cecelia; and Tim, Tyler, Conner, Noah, McCall and Oliver.

Most of all, I thank God for my whole life and His greatest gift to me, which will be my eternal life through Christ Jesus.

Quotes of Mine That Have Helped Me with Life

Give up your dreams for anything less and a lifetime passes you by.

What matters to you my thoughts or dreams, for I am called home to only me?

Walk away with a frown and a frown leads your way.

The beauty of death is lost to the terrible pain in our hearts.

My first poems, starting around third grade had innocence, yet captured an early understanding of what was important to me at such a tender age.

As I grew older, my poems took on more mature subjects but still remained easy to read. My life took on more meaning and substance, and therefore, my poetry did too. I began including religion and world events in my small, thoughtful poems.

Our Kind of Day

Out in the meadow,
We were one day.
Looking for cows
And just to play.

It wasn't a day
For being in the house;
Not when you could play
And look for cows!

A Snuggly Teddy Bear

A Snuggly Teddy bear

Every time I see a truck,

Especially a milk truck

I always think of a little bear,

A snuggly teddy bear.

Umbrella Tree

Umbrella tree,

Cool, autumn breeze,

Rust-colored leaves,

Waving good-bye to summer.

🌿 A Puff of White 🌿

A puff of white

In a sky of blue

Is pollution to some.

To me?

It's a marshmallow kite!

How about you?

How Are You Today?

Hi there!
How are you today?

See here!
Have you lost your way?

Don't fear!
Why not stay with me a day?

Hey there!
Tomorrow is another day.

Snow Is a Miracle

It was snowing when I awoke today
Swirling so softly to the ground.

A wonderful way to start the day
White, shining loveliness all around.

Snow is a miracle, wouldn't you say?
It falls clear from heaven, not making a sound.

On Learning to Read

Life began when I was born,
    In the winter so forlorn.

The youngest of six, the baby,
    And forever my nickname: Baby.

Everyone petted and loved me so—
    I was pampered all day from head to toe.

My sisters set my hair in pin curls,
    And soon I became a daddy's girl!

Me and my yellow angora cat stayed
    In a white picket fence, where we played.

The family said I used to ride our cow;
    If so, I really don't remember how.

When I was around six, school began;
    All in plaid, down the driveway I ran.

School was nice, and first grade flew past!
    My life at seven was moving real fast.

A new world just opened and planted a seed;
    For now, you see, I was learning to read.

I read with zest for my young age,
    For I found something new page after page.

My passion for reading has never gone:
    Now at eight, I read from dawn to dawn!

The Joy of Books!

Books line the shelves
Like
Flowers in a garden.

One high, one low,
Some
Bending to and fro,

Waiting there for our enjoyment!
Oh—
What joy they bring!

Glorious Green

Light and bouncy days of spring,
Wrap me in your arms of green.

Please, oh please, come and bring
Your blossoms and your glorious green.

Write Me Sometime

If across the miles was only a few,
　　We would brunch and hunch;
　　Have lunches together.

Rather, it is many miles, plus a few.
　　So, we mean to write and call
　　But, procrastinate together.

When the Sun Begins to Show

On a dreary rainy day
The sun is away.

Clouds linger close to the sea
Where can the sun be?

Yes, on a cloudy day, the sun is missed—
Terribly missed!

So, when the sun begins to show,
All faces, too, begin to glow!

Mushrooms

Mushrooms

And when it rains

Mushrooms become umbrellas

For all sorts of tiny creatures.

I guess God planned it that way.

Progress?

New houses rising
On fields—I used to sing,
And skinny dip
And run and skip.

Now the trees are downed,
The creek underground;
I wish my fields
Were once more fields.

Tara

Tara is our little girl:

She's all ready to unfurl

Just like a spring day

In the month of May.

Page of Poems

If my kisses were
Merely pages
And my love for
You, poems,

I would shower you
With pages
Brimming full
Of poems.

Royal Mountains, Loyal Valleys

Royal Mountains, Loyal Valleys

Ah! The mountains!
    Gifts from God: royal,
    Serene, and stately.
    Rising above, yet loyal
    To the fertile valley,
    Feeding it with soil
    And water daily.

And in return, the valley
    Lies in wait to return
    Fertile soil and abundant
    Water, giving patiently
    All things back
    To the mountains, gladly,
    Tenderly and faithfully.

Their Time Ago

Yes we were young
A time ago.
We ran and jumped
Were on the go.

How free and easy
The days went by;
Cold, rain or snow,
We never asked why.

Nice clothes, clean clothes,
Who thought or cared?
Mud pies, fireflies—
Whatever we dared!

And oh, so quaint,
As sayings go,
Now our kids are in
"Their time ago."

My Sandpiper

A sandpiper took a walk
    --With me!
Down to the shore
    --Beside the sea.
He stayed just ahead
    --A little afraid,
I stooped to pick a shell
    --He waited, one legged.
Our world seemed small
    --Just he and I,
Then he flew away
    --Now just I.

The Apple Tree and Moon Beyond

The Apple Tree

I sat and watched the apple tree
The moon was just beyond.

You'll never guess what it meant to me:
It made me sad and gay, for I longed

To be as calm as that apple tree
And as free as the moon beyond.

Indian Summer

Watch closely for the signs.

The afternoon shadows will take on a deeper shade of green

The flowers will look stark against the other, fading foliage,

And the heat of summer will begin to wane.

As the dread of winter looms--oh, so near

Just as the leaves put on their color supreme,

Suddenly you realize Indian summer is peeking round the corner.

He Is God's Child, Not Mine

Oh God,
      I've held this hand in mine
      So long against thy will;
      I've guided it,
      Washed it,
      Kissed it,
      Taught it—loved it so.
      Still, something is missing.

Now God,
      Unwillingly, but knowingly,
      I'll slip it into yours at last.
      I give it up not easily,
      Even regretfully
      And sobbingly;
      I was ill-equipped to hold it at all,
      And now I mustn't any longer.

For God, I've learned
      My son is Yours to care for, and
      You've been waiting all this time.

# Helvetia, WV

Quaint, this village of Helvetia,
Reminiscent of a quieter, more
Gentle way of life. Not less work
But, more a joy of living. A working
Place where staying alive could have
Become a tedious, repetitious
Series of tasks: canning, quilting,
Wood chopping, and spinning just to
Survive the winters, rather it became
Instinct; somehow, a knowing need
Of celebration; a time for coming
Together; work at hand mingling
With indestructible spirit, fun, survival,
And, most of all, true love of God.

*(A lovely little Swiss town in WV close to where my father grew up high
above in the logging community of Silica. Some of our relatives helped
settle this area in the mid 1800's and where we still maintain a small
cabin so the grandchildren and all of us can spend time in wonderful
Helvetia.)*

Shot Down Again

And when down-hearted,
Not understood by the world
It may seem—

One tries, tries, and tries only
To hit upon another, non-caring
Lazy person.

The minorities got their equal rights,
Women's libbers theirs, but,
What's it mean?

Hopefully, more to them
Than to an honest worker,
Shot down again!

Winter Tapestry

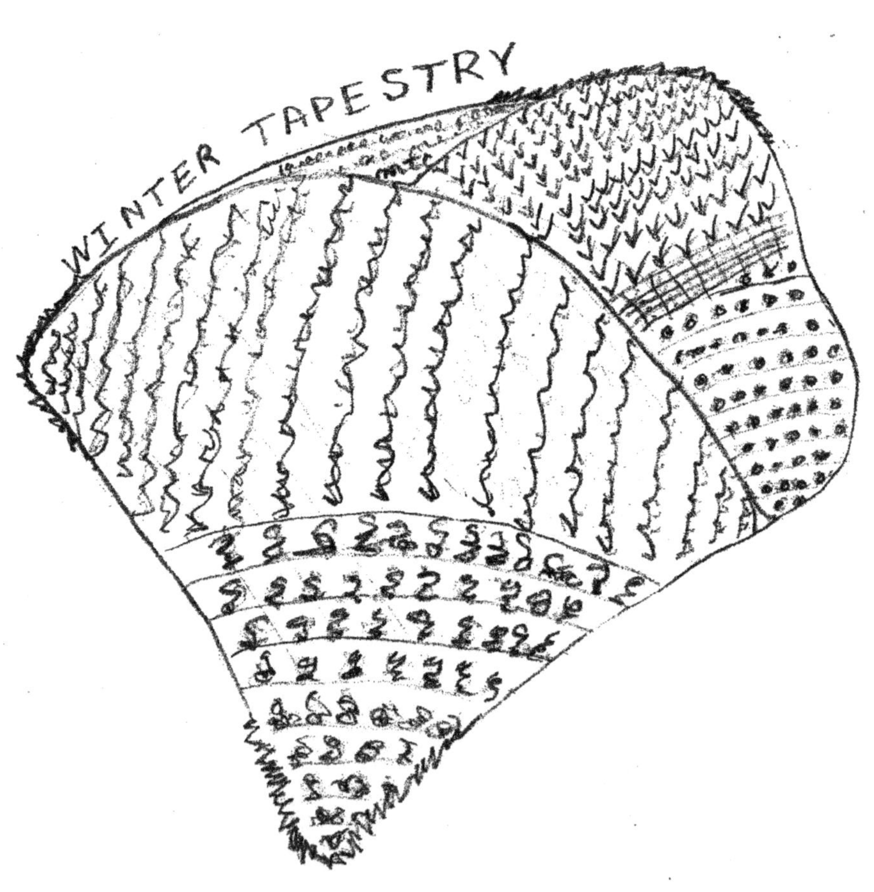

Winter Tapestry

The world is a cozy blanket today
    Woven in shades of green, grey
And brown: a tapestry day,
    Wintery, making the edges to fray.

The snow and the weeds
    Form tweed in the fields.
Lace and crochet each windowpane fill.
    God tucked us in, now all is still.

On Responsibility

You can pass the buck,

Try to change your luck,

Or just say, "Ah, shucks."

But, a responsibility truly yours

You won't be able to duck!

Do You Remember?

Do you remember little cups of ice cream
With little wooden spoons?

Do you remember making authentic mud food,
Fruit pies and spaghetti rolled just right?

Do you remember trying for hours to climb upon a cow?
But poor old Bessie repeatedly moved aside.

Do you remember the bread man driving in your drive
With a truck full of goodies, umm, devil dogs?

Do you remember how wonderful you felt at the tippy
Top of a tree swaying gently in the breeze?

Do you remember being hot and tired coming in for a
Cool bath, fresh jammies and bed?

Do you remember not being able to stop giggling
Then floating away into a quiet, dreamy sleep?

Do you remember how easy it was just being a child?

Dear God?

Death and its torment
Belong to us who stay.

Beauty and contentment
To those who pass away.

God, let us forget the torment
And feel your contentment always.

Amen

❧ Mothers Day Breakfast ☙

"Mom! Hey Mom! Tell us where the skillet could be
And we'll fix you breakfast in bed you see."

"Oh, we found it; please go back to sleep—
It'll just be a minute cause Dad's gonna help."

I sink under the covers, oh, what a thrill;
A crash in the kitchen brings me out with a chill!

"Sorry Mom. Hey Mom, just go back to sleep.
Now be quiet so Mom can sleep—not a peep."

The aroma of bacon drifts passed my nose;
The thought of this treat makes me wiggle my toes.

To be awakened suddenly: "No! She likes scrambled!
No! An omelet!" Uh oh! Once over scrambled?

"Oh! The toast—get—SOMEONE GET THE TOAST!!
It's burnt a little, no matter, she likes dark toast."

My nerves are shattered, sleep? A thing of the past.
"Get the juice, a napkin, Mommy, sit up fast."

Anticipation swells all over my being—"HEY!"
Just as the flowers spill all over my tray.

With squeals of happiness, delight and surprise
My Mother's Day breakfast finally arrives.

A tray filled with love from my family to me!
"Mom, we really wanted to surprise you, did we?"

God Taught Us All

I watched in silent wonder as

A maple tree wrapped its strong arms

Around an evergreen tree.

It held the young tree gently against

The harsh, gusty spring time storm.

Then in thanks

When the sun came out

The evergreen spread

Its branches wide

Shading the roots of the maple tree.

Fireworks!

A brilliant show of fireworks

Displayed itself on my yard today!

The colors were spectacular;

From sunshine yellow

To a gold so pure, refined

I thought of sparkling nuggets

As one dandelion after another

Burst forth across my yard!

Dancing Timber

The Dance Of The Timber

The timber stood majestically
    So tall, so straight, so bold.
Then all at once the wind began,
    First slight, then to behold.

And as the wind pounced on the trees
    A symphony began to play.
Little trees in front leaped left, but
    The stouter timber stood their stay.

But movement began way in back
    Some saplings bowed to the right.
And leaves left high began to shimmer
    As they caught the morning light.

Sporadically in time to none
    Shorter trees began shacking.
With twinkling light and abandonment
    The timber dance was changing.

Stillness came as if a rest, but just as quickly
    The wind picked up and very soon
With absolute precision and grace
    All timber pranced and danced in tune.

If God Were To Come

It's hard to be good
    Day after day
    Or day after day
To be happy always.

Smiles are not easy
    When you're tired and worn
    And the kids have just torn
Your very best dress.

Happiness does not crest
    When you just mopped
    And everyone flopped
Their mud on your floor.

But If God were to come
    And get you right now
    Please tell me just how
You would face him today?

The Heartfelt Pain
of Mid-Life Crisis

I thought I was immune to the agony of mid-life crisis.
Those feelings of lost youth;
  Tingling skin awash with a
   Glow from a lover's touch.

I thought I was too sensible, too into the present
To ever notice how much of life had passed
  Into yesteryears, gone forever
   With my youth, never to be again.

I thought I would not mind growing older,
Growing more mature, my life fuller
  In many more ways than my youth
   Had ever been, but yet—

I thought I would never miss my youth.
The joys, the freedom, for with that
  There had also been sadness
   And heartaches, through teenage years.

I now believe my thoughts were based on hope
And fears. In not actually knowing how mid-life crisis
  Might make me feel. I thought
   It would not change me, but—

That was before.

Now I know I have arrived at this life-crisis.
I know the fears and feelings of lost youth
  Are real, no matter how sensible I may be,
   The years of my youth are haunting me.

I know I can get through this craziness, recover and go
on as before, but right now my whole being reaches out
  To my youth of long ago
   As it slips away with age.

Thanks be to God

Thanks be to God For
    He has blessed
Us with His infinite,
    Unselfish giving.

He gave us our lives,
    This land east and west,
And bountiful harvests
    Just for the asking.

Above all else He gave
    Us His Son, blessed
Be to Him—let us
    Join in Thanksgiving.

Boys and War

I sat in my living room and watched as two
    Young boys played at war.

The first boy getting his equipment and men
    Set up tight in a line near and far.

Some men huddled in make-shift trenches;
    Others were scattered walking or dead.

Then boy number two maneuvered his tanks
    Rushing and pushing to get them ahead.

Then on swift wing all their planes they
    Brought in, flying up, up very high.

Some planes exploded with each round of shots.
    They created a dramatic display in the sky.

The planes drifted left, then to the right,
    Then fell to death from way up high.

Ah, how the boys loved to play war;
    They didn't understand, I thought with a sigh.

Suddenly, a third boy with great courage and might
    Driving hard, entered this war from the east.

With superior war tanks, planes, and men
    His troops were many and he—a beast!

Stalin had swept in with vengeance and strength,
    trapping Hitler between the Allies and he,

With tears in my eyes for I could not bear it,
    I jumped from my seat and turned off the TV.

A Gift

I cannot write of those who go
    But only those who stay.
I have not gone so cannot say
    How death affects those who go.

The torments, fears and questions:
    Why was he taken?
You must be mistaken!
    God, please answer my questions!

It is hard to face another day,
    To see the sun,
Or ever have fun,
    With loneliness guiding my way.

They say "Turn to God."
    But He took him!
How can I trust Him?
    Not realizing why or how, I turn to God.

I ask Him to help me through this death.
    I am filled with a glow,
And suddenly know
    God's miraculous gift comes with death.

So You Accepted Christ?

So, you accepted Jesus Christ?
I suppose the ground shook
And the wind blew?

I've heard stories of accepting Christ!
How the bells chime
And the sky brightens.

So now you believe in this Christ?
Did your knees collapse?
Did you faint in awe?

Yes, I accepted Jesus Christ.
I believe the day was gloomy
And remained gloomy.

My life now belongs to Christ.
But there were no outright
Signs and the weather? Unimportant!

I have joy in my heart—from Christ.
You see, His promise was
Eternal life, not earthquakes
And chiming bells!

Writing short, thought-provoking articles is

something I have done throughout my life. I often use

scriptures from the Bible to help illustrate situations

taking place at the time of my writings.

As Easter Approaches

Easter is fast approaching and as you begin your Easter preparations, plan on sending *more* than an Easter Card to friends and relatives.

There are so many people that each of us care about, but, unfortunately we don't seem to care whether they go to heaven or not. Sharing the plan of salvation with a friend is probably the last thing we would ever think of doing, yet it is the very reason God placed us on His earth. We fear losing friendships, we are embarrassed, or we just don't know how to actually share the plan of salvation. When we decide we want to we can overcome each and every excuse. For instance, if our fear is losing a friend, what a small price to pay: losing a friend to God.

As you buy your cards for Easter, the celebration of Christ's Resurrection, remember to send more than an Easter card, send the plan of salvation. If you are not comfortable with how it goes, Romans 10: 8-13 (some call the Roman Road) gives the complete plan of salvation. Read it, write it, and send it!

EMPTY

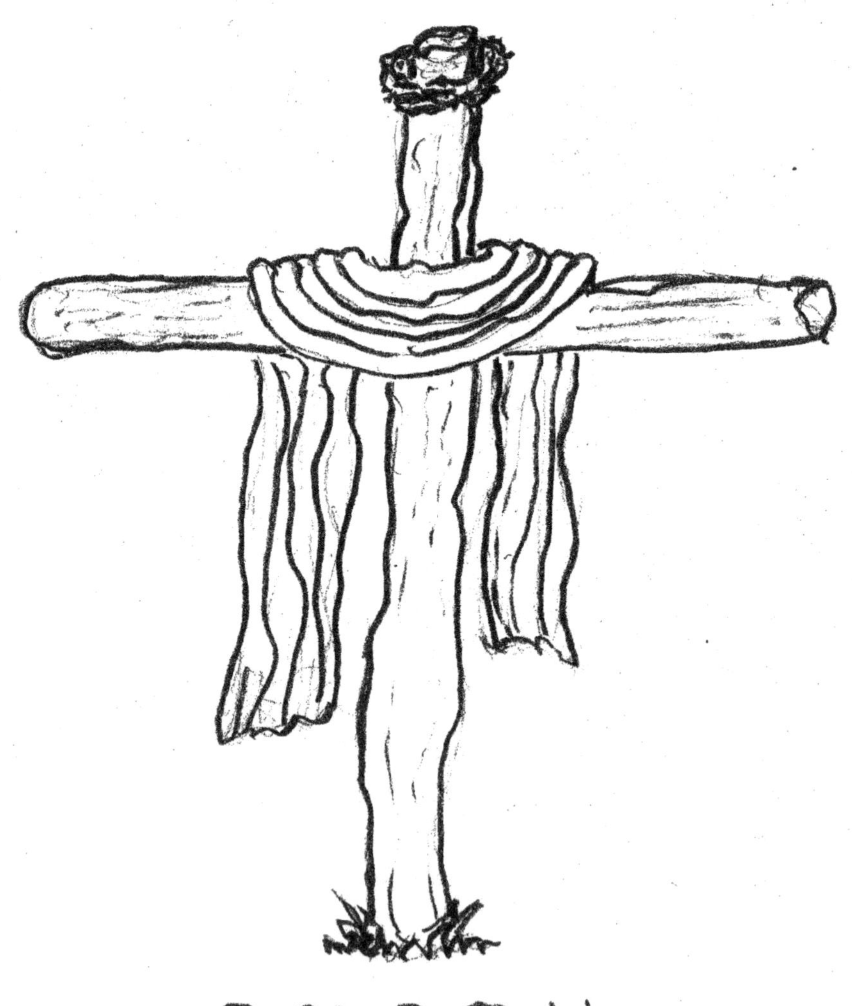

Hallelujah, Christ Arose!

Over the Easter Holiday the words of a much loved song, "Christ the Lord is Risen Today," come alive to me; I want to share my thoughts from the first verse of this glorious song:

"Up from the grave He arose,"

What a miraculous moment for Jesus' followers realizing all He said IS true.

"With a mighty triumph o'er His foes,"

At long last His followers knew they had won over Satan. The cross is empty.

"He arose a victor from the dark domain,"

For Jesus ascended to Heaven: the grave could not hold Him! The tomb is empty.

"And He lives forever with His saints to reign."

We, the believers will reign with Jesus.

HALLELUJAH! Christ Arose!

I Chose The Bumpy Road. . .

When I was sixteen I attended a revival meeting at a church in my neighborhood. Emotions in the crowd ranged from gentle tears to agonizing sighs as the minister warned of impending danger, the fire of hell, and the ultimate payment. I was in awe! My eyes and ears could not take it all in fast enough. I remember feeling a gentle touch nudging me, pushing me toward the front of the church.

I did not go to the front of the church that evening. I did not heed the gentle nudging. I did not want to be embarrassed; after all, there were some older kids from school sitting nearby. What would they think? I just could not take the chance.

I like to believe I really did not understand the minister at that revival. But, that is not true; it is easier than admitting I was so sensitive to what my peers thought that I put their feelings before my own salvation. I chose at age sixteen to take the bumpy road.

You see young friends, God is going to have His way in your life; however, He is a gentleman. He will let you make your life as difficult as you want knowing in the end He will have the final say. The difference? His way is smoother, easier, and nicer while your way is full of self-doubt, emptiness, loneliness, and possibly much worse.

You say, "Oh, no, not with all my friends, I could never be lonely." Don't believe it! You will experience loneliness and hurt from your friends because they are human. On God's smooth road you will never be alone for He walks His road with you: God never deserts His children. Hebrews 13: 5 "...I will never desert you, nor will I ever forsake you..."

I am not telling you what to do, I am only sharing with you what I experienced while travelling the bumpy road. I want you to know how much more God might have used me had I been wise enough to choose His way rather than my way. It hurts me to think of all the time I wasted dodging pot-holes when I could have been gently guided along God's road doing His will.

Which way? Which road will you travel? I pray you will choose God's road.

Sitting With Mom

All day I sat quietly beside the hospital bed where my mother lay sleeping. She, at eighty years old, awaiting heart catheterization and possibly open-heart surgery, I, waiting to say the right words to her, words that would encourage her through the upcoming days. Yet, my thoughts would not rest on today, but rather drifted back to my childhood, to a time when my mother was in control of me. A time when I waited for her to fix my breakfast, comb my hair, sew my dress or tell me what to do.

It was so easy to be under my mom's control, easy on me. Now I am supposed to be in control—and I am uncomfortable with the change in positions. For all I want to do right now is climb on my mom's lap and cry softly into her shoulder cause, "mom, right now I ache for you so very, very much."

When You Lose
Someone You Love

My life just experienced an awful tragedy: my mother, bless her heart, has gone home forever. She went into the hospital for heart surgery and had a massive stroke during the surgery. The doctors were optimistic for a day or two so we, my brother and sisters, spent all day every day with mom hoping above all else she could at least hear our voices; the doctors assured us she could. So, we talked and prayed and cried just as if she were awake and spending the day at one of our homes.

Three thoughts kept me going, **mom is saved,** and, **at long last she will hold her firstborn, the wee child who died in her womb.** But, most of all, because I so wanted mom to live awhile longer I kept reminding myself of the Bible verse, **"Be still, and know that I am God."** Psalm 46:10

Separate Ourselves From The Bible?

Coming down our stairway one morning, I noticed a red glow coming from the kitchen. It was lovely and from past experience I knew there was a magnificent, red sunrise awaiting me.

As I stared in wonder at the sunrise the little "sailor's verse" ran through my mind, "Red sails at night; sailor's delight. Red sails at morning; sailors take warning." I must have said that verse hundreds of times since first hearing it as a child and I always wondered which sailor had written it. But, just recently I discovered where it actually came from: the Bible.

Matthew 16:2, 3 "…when it is evening, you say, 'It will be fair weather, for the sky is red.' And in the morning, 'There will be a storm today, for the sky is red and threatening'…"

It seems strange to me, with the recent controversy over separation of church from just about everything, that many of our beliefs, habits, customs, traditions, and even quotations originally came from that which we are to separate ourselves??

Use Jesus As Your Safety Valve

Did you ever see someone over-dressed for an occasion or over-reacting to a simple situation? What was your first impression of that person? Did you say, "Oh well, they probably didn't know any better." No, I'll bet your thoughts were more like, "Who do they think they are all fixed up? Or, "What is his problem?"

Discretion means the quality of being discreet, or being careful about what one does and says. There are many verses in the Bible that speak of discretion. Why? Because first opinions are very important and God desires us to always set an example befitting one of His children. If our clothes and/or actions demonstrate gaudiness or a slovenly manner, most people will never see past that to know our hearts belong to God.

No one is 100 percent accurate about being discreet, for everyone's tastes are different. But, there is a way to learn to use discretion: simply use Jesus as a safety valve. For instance, someone is giving you a tongue-lashing at work, you are all ready to holler back, when, suddenly your relief valve opens and you see Jesus in the same situation. What does He do? That is the easy part, for we all know how Jesus would behave. The hard part is to mimic Him. So, the more we put the safety valve theory into use, the more we will be able to practice discretion.

Philippians 1:9, 10 say, "And this I pray, that your love may abound still more and more in real knowledge and all discernment, so that you may approve the things that are excellent, in order to be sincere and blameless until the day of Christ."

Happy Every Holiday!

What can each of us do to keep Valentine's Day going all year long? The Spirit of Christmas? The Triumphant Joy of Easter?

First, we must determine what all these holidays have in common. Yes, they are all holidays, but what is it about a holiday that gives everyone such a good feeling?

Holidays are days of giving and sharing love; a celebration of love. They are days when many people give and receive gifts; a thoughtful day. They are days set apart from all the rest; a special day. So, you might say holidays are a celebration of love and thoughtfulness on a very special day.

When we celebrate the birth of Jesus Christ is it not a celebration of love?

> I John 4:10 "Herein is love, not that we loved God, but that He loved us, and sent His Son to be the propitiation for our sins."

When we celebrate Easter is it not a celebration of love?

> John 3:16 "For God so loved the world that He gave His only begotten Son, that whosoever believeth in Him should not perish, but have everlasting life."

A holiday is a special day, a day set aside to celebrate the love of God. It is the love of God that all holidays have in common. We are actually celebrating the love of God in one form or another. Must we have a special day to celebrate God's love? No. We can keep the Valentine's

Day spirit going or have Christmas all year long by remembering:
I John 4:16 "… God is love…"

Every day of the year we can simply think, 'Today is a special day because God loves me.' This one thought should give you the joy of all the holidays rolled into each and every day, all year long.

Happy Every Holiday…All Year Long!

A Protective Wall

Did you ever think how nice it would be if you could keep all your loved ones in a protected area where they would always be safe? Unfortunately, it is impossible. And even if you could, they probably would not like it, nor would they stay in your restricted area.

Let me share a thought: you can still put your loved ones in a protected area, actually inside a wall, without their even knowing.

This wall is an invisible barrier which would let all life's normal trials and tribulations enter, but all persons inside this wall would possess the God given strength to better handle all of the ups and downs of everyday life.

In Job 1:10 Satan, speaking to God acknowledges a wall of protection. "Have you not put a hedge around him and his household and everything he has?" Even Satan knew of the power God provides to those inside this invisible wall.

So, go ahead, pray your loved ones inside a protective wall where God issues all the necessary artillery to hold strong against the enemy.

The Strange Summer of 1988

I don't really understand why, but the summer of 1988 was very strange:

- Heat high enough to make the nicest person turn into a raging maniac at the drop of a pin,

- So little rain that our farms turned to dust fields rather than corn fields,

- People getting sick with very different illnesses: pancreatic diseases, blood clots in the lungs, etc.,

- Even the skunks and raccoons developed an illness whereby they acted tame but were actually very sick and contagious to farm animals, pets, and people!

My mind went crazy trying to think of a reason for these happenings, let alone all the other crazy things going on around the world.

Because the Bible says strange things will happen near the end of time, over the years, one group or another has said "the end of time is coming soon." Maybe there truly were other times in history when as many odd things occurred at the same time, I don't know, but I do know this has been the oddest year in my memory. It makes me wonder, is it the end of time?

God's Truths are in the Bible

Through the years there have been movies made in Hollywood that have not gone along with the teachings of the Bible. One of these movies, "The Last Temptation," created quite a stir. I did not see the movie, so I am unable to give an opinion; however, I would like to give the public something to think about concerning things not of the Bible. No matter what religion you are, no matter what you believe in your life, you have some level of intelligence and should be able to discern, to some extent, what is or is not hype.

If it is hype, label it so. If you cannot really decide, study what is available to you and then make a decision based upon your findings, rather than the idea(s) of a small group of creative people.

Most importantly, pray to God for direction and understanding while reading His word, the Bible, as He reveals His truths to you.

God's Ultimate Gift

Everything we have God gave us. He first gave a place for us to be: the Earth. He then gave us life filled with riches untold. But, His ultimate gift to all who believe: His son, Christ Jesus.

Therefore, we should humble ourselves and accept Jesus as our Saviour, thereby reaping the benefit of God's final gift: Eternal life in Heaven with Him.

She Loves Me, She Loves Me Not

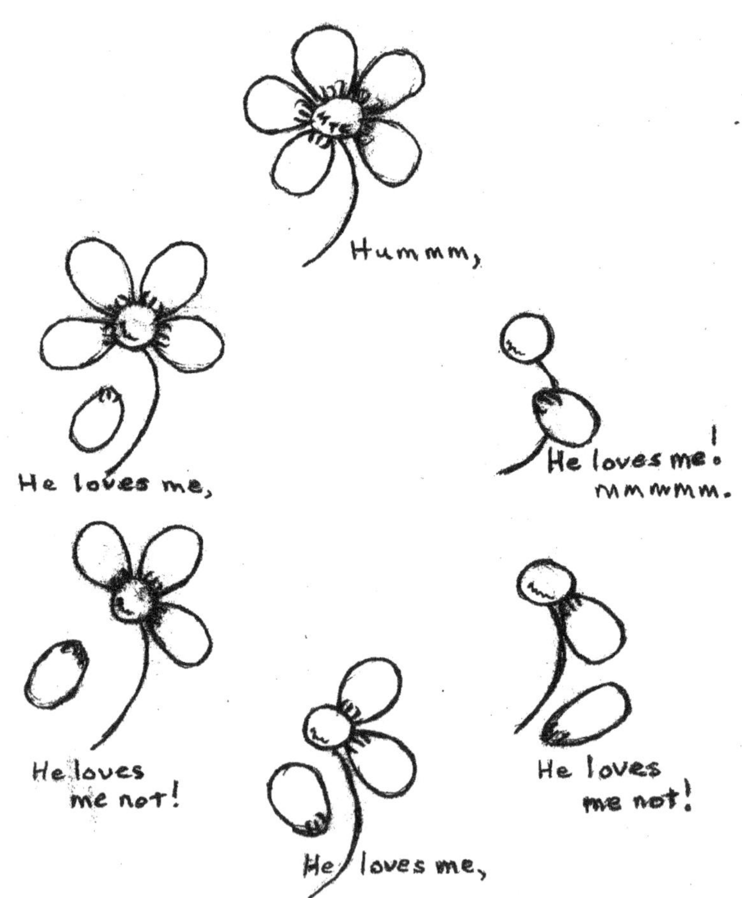

She Loves Me, She Loves Me Not

Although love is one of the most powerful human emotions, it is also one of the most uncertain. Because of this uncertainty people through the ages have tried many ways to learn about 'love.' Medieval sorcerers used magic, herbs, and spices to find lovers' answers. Shakespearean characters plucked petals from flowers, with each fallen petal a sign of affection or none. Alas, only when one petal remained was the true answer known.

Thanks to God we have a better way to learn of love. The Bible gives many verses dealing with love. There is the great book of love: The Songs of Solomon. And in Ephesians 5 and 6 there are special words to a loving wife and husband on how the relationship of a family should be.

Pick a day, any day and share a verse with someone you care about from God's great Book of Love, The Songs of Solomon.

Tornado Season and Spring

Tornado season is upon us; a time of fear, apprehension, pain, and sorrow. The guidelines for living through a tornado are readily available. Warnings can be seen moving quickly across the bottom of our TV screens as the 'season' sets in for its too-long stay.

But also, the season of spring is fast approaching; spring, a time of renewal, beauty, hope, and happiness. Soon, signs of spring will be everywhere: pussy willows, robins, and most of all warmer weather.

The Bible, in Ecclesiastes 3:1-8 tells of a time for all things. God intended the tornado season and the spring season to coincide. Why? We do not know the answer, but are reminded in Romans 8:28, "all things work together for good to those who love God."

Nature is not an accident. I believe God put these two unlike times together, encouraging us through tornado season with the great expectancy of spring.

Share The Word Of God

I have learned my main purpose according to God's plan is to share the word of God. This involves witnessing, which for some of us is hard to do so we do not do it.

There are a number of reasons for not witnessing, from shyness to actually knowing, but not admitting that we are not Christians. My excuse fell somewhere in between.

As a new Christian I thought I did not know enough about the Bible and God to witness; therefore, I would not witness until I learned all about the Bible and God. This excuse would let me off the hook for a long time.

God had other plans, for soon people began asking me Biblical questions. I tried to put them off, but more came until finally I went to my pastor and asked what to do.

"Plant seeds," he said, "just plant one seed at a time and let God handle it from there, He will nurture it along."

So, I began to plant seeds, just a word, a thought, a verse, and no heavy lectures. The more seeds I planted, the more questions were asked of me until the seeds that were needed became impossible to carry. Give up? Never! So, I prayed, "God, please send me a John Deere Planter!"

(Pastor Robert Combs of Grace Church, Norton, Ohio was the one who offered this great piece of advice that I have used ever since he gave it to me.)

A Less Than Perfect Society

The foreign gentleman on the TV commercial who "loves this country" because he got "best chicken" in a fish place shows one of many contradictions in this life of ours. Some other ones are much less fun than the chicken commercial.

For instance, we declare a National Day of Recognition for one man, and manage to get another man to drop out of the race for the presidency, both men, supposedly having similar life styles. Or a happening in a small town where twelve to fifteen year old children were literally run out of a world-wide hamburger place (which is kids-oriented) while bars in this same town flung wide their doors to the under aged. These are only a few examples of oddities in this great country where we live.

Why, in a democracy where there are two and three laws to cover just about every situation a person could imagine, are there so many contradictions? Well, it is quite simple: this great country is now, always has been, and always will be run by human beings. And, although I know this will surprise most everyone, human beings are not always correct in their thoughts and actions. Try as we might, we are a less than perfect society.

There will be a time when justice will be carried out perfectly. A time when every judgment will be exactly correct and the punishments will always be appropriate. Think, if you will, about that great day when Christ comes back to rule the earth for 1,000 years. Rev. 20: 4-7 says "There never could be a better ruler, for Christ is perfect."

Until that wondrous day, we must do our best to live at peace in a less than peaceful world. Remembering that to God, each person is unique, valuable, and has the ability, with His help, to make our world a better place.

Voting Our Responsibility?

For years I went about during times of election bragging of my lack of interest in voting: my vote won't count, good people change when they get into office, and politicians are only out for themselves.

Then one day I read Hebrews 13:17 "Obey your leaders and submit to them. . ." The verse would not let me rest; I felt a guilt I did not understand.

I tried to rationalize my non-voting once again; however, the odd, nagging guilt would not go away. I understood from Hebrews that God told me to obey my leaders, but how could He expect me to do that unless I took an active roll in picking the very best leader possible? So God was giving me this responsibility and the only way to accomplish it is to pray and then vote.

Our founding fathers set up our government in such a way that we each can have a voice in every election. They believed in God and based our constitution on their beliefs. We each should be honored to be a part of such an important process and take voting as a responsibility honoring our forefathers and our God.

When To Pray?

The heat has been unbelievable for the past two weeks: much of the United States is in the throes of the worst drought since 1905.

As in other desperate times there are people saying, "The end is near, prepare for the end of times." Others pay little attention to the heat, going about their business as usual. A few, those especially affected by the drought are worried, maybe even scared!

These frightened people, in their hour of need, are turning to God. Many farmers in Northeastern Ohio gathered recently in a dry, barren corn field to pray for rain. The weather report did not call for rain that day, or the next, or even that week. Those people were not pleased with the weather report, so they simply went over the weatherman's head speaking directly to God.

Did they get the rain they prayed for?

I think a much more important question to ask is: if they had been praying all along, the way God asks, would there have been a drought?

We The People Need To Pray Without Ceasing

We have no other course of action—that is why the presidential candidates campaign so hatefully. They know one of them will become president with or without each of our votes.

We may dislike the way they conduct themselves; we may hate the way they smear mud in each others' faces; we may even despise their lies; three major actions we teach our children NOT to do. But, no matter how these grown men or women act, the fact remains one of them will become our next president. At which point we will be expected to believe, follow, and support their every move.

I think "We, the people of the United States, in order to form a more perfect nation" should pray without ceasing for more and better courses of action.

Spring Break At The Ocean

It seems to be a ritual that high school seniors must go to some ocean for their last spring break.

This year I hope they *only* go to see and enjoy one of God's greatest creations: the ocean.

There are no words to explain the wonder of all that water lightly caressing the sand; ebbing out, only to come tumbling or at times, crashing back to shore.

The fragrance and gentleness of the sea breezes delight the senses. And the seagulls appear whiter and call more musically than ever imagined.

When the time comes to leave, sadness takes hold of every emotion; but the beauty and majesty of the ocean remain in one's heart forever.

More Eternal Value

Did you ever stop to wonder what you might be doing five years from now? Ten years from now?

Do you have goals set in place to obtain your desires?

Take some time to assess your future plans, write them down. Then cross out every plan that has no eternal (heavenly) value.

Ask yourself, "What must I change in my life to gain more eternal value?"

The Story of Christmas

'And it came to pass in those days, a decree went out from Caesar Augustus, that all the world should be taxed.

And Joseph went to be taxed in the city of David, Bethlehem, with Mary his wife, being great with child.

And so it was, that, while they were there, the days were accomplished that she should be delivered.

And she brought forth her first born son, and wrapped him in swaddling clothes, and laid him in a manger; because there was no room for them in the inn.

And in the same country shepherds abiding their flocks were come upon by an angel of the Lord saying, "Fear not: for, behold, I bring you tidings of great joy. For unto you is born a Saviour which is Christ, the Lord."'

And so, Jesus Christ, our Saviour became the reason for all Christmas Seasons, then, now, and forever. Amen. Luke 2:1-11

New Years Resolutions

Nineteen eighty-nine: the year I vowed to write more notes to others, send birthday cards—on time, and join a gymnastics class; 1989, the year I did none of the above. Instead, 1989 was a year of adjustment; trying to step gracefully into the older generation after the sorrowful loss of my mom; changing my role of 'mommy' to my little boy who came home from high school graduation a young man; attempting a major makeover in my personal life through a Bible study on becoming a woman of excellence.

By Christmas I had wanted 1989 all straightened and ready to be filed away; however, there seemed to be loose ends sticking out all over. The Bible in Ecclesiastes 3:1 says, "There is an appointed time for everything." This means I must be mismanaging my time so, I vow to better use my God-given time next year.

And going on past performance, I will be able to save some time by using this same article next year.

HO-HO-HO and Happy New Year!

In Search of Excellence

We use the word excellence, but very seldom in connection with ourselves. The Bible; however, often speaks of obtaining excellence in our Christian lives. Here are some ways to begin the search for excellence:

1. Think only good thoughts; we become what we think. (Philippians 4:8)

2. Strive for the greater gifts; the way will be shown. (I Corinthians 12:31)

3. Pray for real knowledge and discernment; we cannot gain excellence if it is unrecognizable. (Philippians 1:9-10)

Study these texts and try with all your heart to entwine them into your life; strive for excellence.

I Can Only Work On Myself

"Hey! I work too. Why should you be able to take a nap before dinner while I, on the other hand, have to prepare dinner? It is NOT fair!" His or her complaint countered with the other's answer, "Because I have a much harder job than you, I actually work all day while you merely sit at a desk!"

This debate has been going on since time began. A program on the radio said it is one of the most frequent arguments in the American home. The next part of the program suggested how to handle the situation: what a shock I received, after all, I knew I was right! They said the argument shows a selfish attitude on both sides. Surprised? We all believe we are the correct one and just in case we might be a little wrong we say, "Well, if they will stop being selfish, so will I." And the battle goes on.

It is easy for us to blame our mate and insist they be the first to change their ways; it is another story to accept blame, apologize, and begin trying to change ourselves. But this is exactly what God would have us do. Remember the verse in the Bible, Matthew 7:6 "You hypocrite, first take the log out of your own eye, and then you will see clearly to take the speck out of your brother's eye."? In other words we need to work on our own lives before directing other people.

Try, by asking the Holy Spirit to bring to your attention daily any selfish viewpoints you might have. Once you become aware of these unwanted attitudes it will be easier to adjust them. Get ready though, because I did this and the nice little me was astounded by the habits of the selfish little me.

He Became Older, I Younger and Wiser.

Growing up as the youngest in a family of six children provided me knowledge the older ones could not understand. For I, in a way, shared in their fun by listening to each little thing they said about everything. But I longed for the day I would be old enough to actually participate in all their daily activities.

I loved winter so the anticipation throughout my childhood of one day being included in the sledding parties back on the hill was more than I could bear at times. However, by the suitable-to-be-with-adults age of fifteen all my brothers and sisters were out of school, some with little ones of their own.

My youngest child, now fifteen, is experiencing this same dilemma. So, last night he and I went out to share an adventure in the snow. I showed him where my cave once was and he, very secretively, pointed in the 'general' direction of his fort. We fell in drifts, slid down (what I remembered as) hazardous cliffs, and talked about fifteen year-old problems in my day and now.

As the evening went on, he became older, and I, younger and wiser.

Christmas Is Jesus' Birthday

Once upon a time there was a young boy who lived in a simple, working class neighborhood. This boy was not disliked, but not especially liked either. In fact, most people did not think anything of the boy at all.

The boy on the other hand, liked everyone very much; he thought of everyone he knew as family. If any of his neighbors needed help of any kind the boy was always there to help. He liked everyone so much that each year on his birthday he invited all his neighbors and friends to help celebrate the day; anyone and everyone was welcome. They attended his party even though most people did not care one way or the other about the boy; after all, there was food and a fun-filled time.

The boy grew into a man and his birthday was still celebrated by all his old friends and neighbors. It had become a traditional party with or without the original birthday boy in attendance!

Does this seem like a strange story? It is a strange story! For who celebrates someone's birthday when they have no personal connection to that person?

Please think of this story as Christmas approaches and if you have no personal connection to Jesus, how about changing that right now, this year, before Christmas?

Romans 10:8-13 gives the plan of salvation, read it and take it to heart, then join in the joyous celebration remembering that **Christmas is Jesus' birthday.**

For A Friend Such As You

At a time in my life when laughter came hard;
You brought me uncontrollable laughter.

Dreading tomorrows as if death were looming;
You made my tomorrows a thing of the past.

Misunderstood, my kindness mistaken by others;
You accepted my kindness and repaid it in full.

Longing for someone to talk with and learn from;
You shared knowledge far beyond your years.

Lacking a friend to share with, have clams with;
You accepted my friendship—even the clams!

Through your clear and innocent young mind
My world became kinder, softer and brighter.

From your friendship, kindness and caring,
My world became better than ever before.

I don't remember just how our friendship began,
But I thank God for a friend such as you.

Under A Sea Of Glistening Clouds

The wind blows and the grass laps at the edge of a field. Golden fingers create waves as one melts into another racing this way and that.

The sunbeams shine down as each one brightens a new crest of waves. The light sparkles off each blade of grass making the field into a shimmering display of diamonds.

A moving, never ending motion of light and waves, yet beneath this field are thousands of private creatures, unseen and probably unthought-of.

Wonder then—are we but tiny creatures under a never ending sea of glistening, blue sky and golden clouds?

If You Truly Believe In God

As the seek button on my car radio paused, I heard a phrase from an old song: "I'll swear there ain't no heaven and I'll pray there ain't no hell."

The phrase stuck with me all day, until finally I stopped pushing it aside and let my mind think its thoughts. My initial thought was that the phrase would perfectly suit a middle-of-the-roader concerning religion. But, after mulling it around a little more my mind changed: first of all, a person must believe in God before heaven or hell enters the picture; and second, if a person professes to believe in God but is not sure there is a heaven or hell, swearing or praying will not alter either.

So, if a person truly believes in God according to His word, the Holy Bible, they would know there is a heaven and a hell. Then, according to this knowledge, they would know not to swear on hell, but relax in the knowledge and joy of the heaven they will one day enter.

...And God Keeps Creating

Sunrise comes with unbelievable colors:
aqua—clear, clean, transparent;
sky blue—bright, bold, heavenly;
pink—light, dainty, powder-like; and
purple—definite, yet iridescent.

They display brilliantly across the eastern sky in such a way you know human hands are not involved with the rippling, the flowing, the churning together.

All the while creating more shades of colors until the number of designs and hues cannot be counted. And all of this changing each second as the sun steadily rises.

Effortlessly God creates spectacular views for our enjoyment. Look up, enjoy, and give thanks to God.

Hallelujah! Christ Arose

"O death, where is thy sting? O grave, where is thy victory?

The sting of death is sin; and the strength of sin is the law.

But thanks be to God, which giveth us the victory through our Lord Jesus

Christ." I Corinthians 15:55-57

Many times in the midst of a difficult situation or just in the course of everyday life we tend to forget Jesus was *crucified* on a cross.

He did not die in agony on the cross due to the terrible deeds He had done; Jesus never sinned. The wrong doing for which He died such a horrifying death was ours; He paid for <u>all of our sins!</u>

Because of the overwhelming love God has for each of us, He created a way for our past, present and future sins to be paid for in full by His Son, our Saviour, Christ Jesus.

If we accept God's gift of Christ Jesus as our Saviour we can glory in the knowledge that OURS is the VICTORY over death.

February, Winter Boredom

Did you ever notice that otherwise tired people have the strength to golf eighteen holes, dance all night or shop through three area malls?

Look at the same people on a workday morning, the dancing marvel can barely get motivated to dress, let alone go to work. The golfer feels his next step may be his last, and the shopping wonder is spent, in more ways than one.

Is it lack of strength? NO! The problem is boredom, a 'disease' that hits all people at different times. Statistics show that mid-winter, February, to be exact, is the worst time of the year for this 'disease' to become active.

February is here and I say let's fight it! From now until spring as we slide out of bed each morning let's grab our Bible and read a Psalm. Then in prayer let's turn our day over to God's care.

I believe this will be our best February ever!

Autumn, The Colorful Season

Autumn is the colorful season; the cool, flannel-shirt time of year. Doesn't that sound good after the extreme heat of the past three months?

The kids, at last, are back in school. Football has begun once more. Both are signs of autumn approaching.

Soon the trees will begin their preparations for fall by closing off their sap and shutting down the store, so to speak. At this time of year the leaves know to dig into their trunks for their warmest, most colorful outfits. This is their time of year; autumn when the leaves put on one of God's most beautiful displays of glorious color.

Our Laws Keep Being Compromised

More and more the laws of our forefathers, laws founded on God's word, are being compromised: the recent TV debates on whether, as a nation, to go deeper into dept, million upon million of God's unborn children being killed each and every day, wars upon wars being fought with no end in sight, and the list goes on and on.

We supposedly fear God on a personal basis when we do wrong—we know it and ask forgiveness. But, on a larger scale do we as a nation fear God? In my opinion we do not! Listen to people around you, they say things like, "As long as they don't bother me, why should I care?" or "That's their own personal problem, not mine!" or "Abortion should be the choice of each woman, after all it is her body."

And our laws keep being compromised.

Maybe the problem is that each of us seldomly recognize all that we do wrong. So little by little all of our combined sins grow into a nation that has forgotten what America was built upon.

Therefore, God's laws, the inspirational laws of our forefathers, become more and more compromised.

On Losing Your Temper

Most everyone has, at one time or another, lost their temper. We know losing our temper is bad for us, still, when we feel we have had enough—boom! That is it!!

Below are two interesting items that may help with your temper:

1. Many studies show that people who quickly lose their tempers also have much higher rates of heart attacks and premature deaths.

2. The Bible teaches us that to lose our temper is a sign of a fool: Proverbs 29:11, "A fool always loses his temper, but a wise man holds it back."

In other words, go forth, my friend, but leave your temper behind.

In-Between Time

In-between time—we are in-between winter and spring. It is not a pleasant time of year. What remains of the snow is dirty and slushy and everywhere else there is mud. The trees are in need of trimming from the blustery, winter storms. No wonder we feel such excitement when the first robin goes hopping across the yard or a crocus pushes up through the snow.

I like to compare this in-between season with new Christians. Ephesians 4:22, 24 say in part, "Lay aside the old self which is being corrupted..." and "...put on the new self, which is in the likeness of God..." Christians still carry signs of their old self, yet, newness is peeping through more and more every day.

II Corinthians 5:17 reads, "Therefore if any man is in Christ, <u>he is a new creature</u>: the old things passed away; behold new things have come."

Winter is passing, behold, spring is bursting forth!

The Star Led The Way

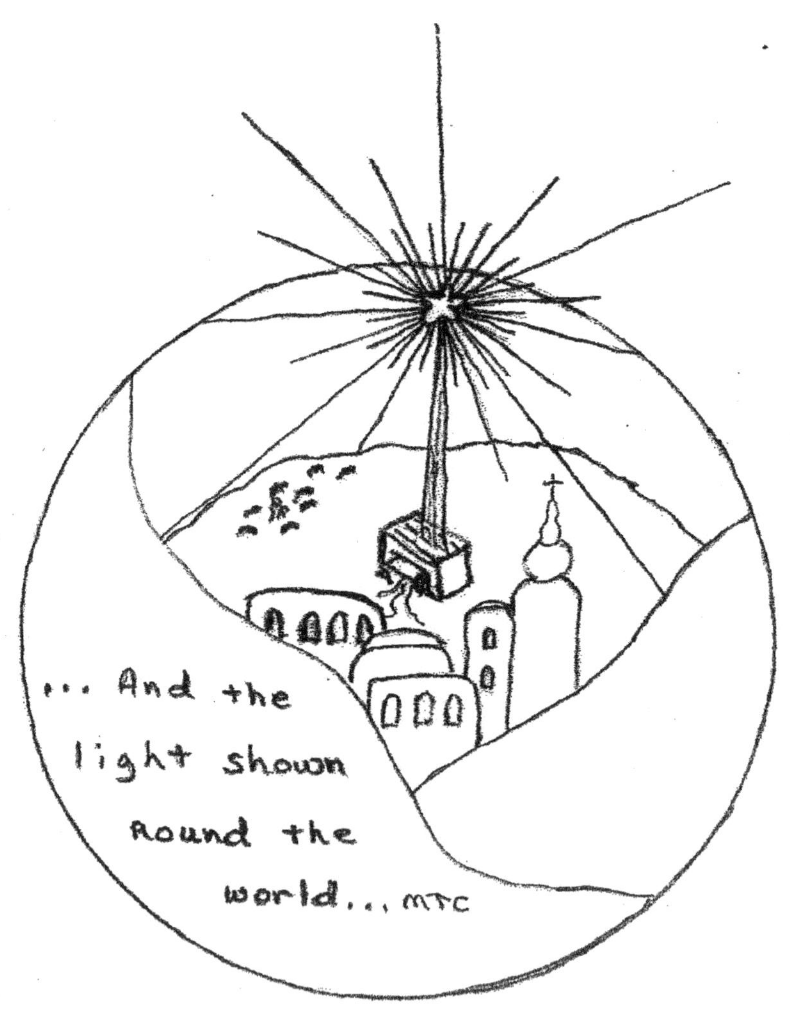

The Star Led The Way

The star led the way to the most wonderful gift we were ever given, our Saviour, Baby Jesus.

You see the great star of wonder and royal beauty led one and all to God's perfect Son.

Prophets foretold the meaning of the glorious star: the Bible says, "…for one star differs from another star in glory."
I Corinthians 15:41

So when the people of the land saw the star shining brightly that night they knew it was a holy night and "they rejoiced exceedingly with great joy." Matthew 2:10

Wise men in far off lands saw the magnificent star in the east and travelled to Bethlehem to worship their Saviour.

Bethlehem was dark, yet in every street, in every corner, in every heart shined the everlasting light of the star of Baby Jesus.

This Christmas Season may each of us realize the true meaning of Christmas and in that tiny spark of truth let a celestial fire be kindled and like the Star of Bethlehem let it lead each and everyone to true peace and eternal life.

A Thought Challenge

Pre-Thanksgiving words are easy, remembering the first Thanksgiving, being thankful for various blessings, etc. However, post-Thanksgiving words are more difficult so rather than recite some flowery speech I want to present you with a thought challenge.

If you believe in the one and only God, the author of our living Bible and the God who created Heaven and earth and each one of us, and sent His only Son to save us from our sins; than I challenge you before the holiday that celebrates the birth of His Son, our Saviour, to think through what has been happening over the past years in relationship to our government and our God. After you think it through, let yourself react to these happenings, write down your thoughts, and experience your gut feelings.

Then pray to our God if there is anything YOU should be doing about these happenings. Search your heart and listen to God and do as he leads.

One person CAN make a difference!

I leave this final thought: remember just one person removed prayer from our schools—is there a noticeable difference in our schools?

Contemplate, read your Bible, pray, and then DO!

Dreams

Around 500 B.C. the Greek philosopher, Heraclitus, spoke of dreams thusly:

> "For the waking there is one common world, but for those asleep, each one retires to his own privacy."

Samuel Taylor Coleridge said of his poem, Kubla Khan, "it was a dream and upon waking I frantically scribbled down between 200 and 300 lines before the dream left my mind."

And more recently Freud observed dreams to be the "Royal Road to the unconscious."

The noun: dream, can mean a sleeping vision, a nightmare, a daydream, a fantasy and more.

The verb: dream can mean the act of daydreaming, to be lost in thought, to think, to consider, to desire, to have a goal and more.

Which brings us full circle to the ending of my book that I shared in the opening a motto I wrote years ago and have honored all of my life:

"Give up your dreams for anything less,
And a lifetime passes you by."

The author, Mildred Thayer Carneal, was born, raised and still lives in the same house in a small Northeastern town in Ohio.

A lifelong desire has been to give poetry that is easy to understand to people just like her. The joy of writing comes from deep feelings about life in general and her personal experiences from childhood, teenage years, being a wife, mother and grandmother, but most of all from becoming a born again Christian. "I thank God for giving me everything I have especially His Son and my Saviour, Christ Jesus."

www.ingramcontent.com/pod-product-compliance
Lightning Source LLC
Chambersburg PA
CBHW040807150726
48196CB00057B/1447